Sparrow, Eagle
Penguin, and Seagull

For my friends at St. Christopher School
in Rocky River, Ohio
—B.P.C.

To my son, Louis-Simon, with all my love.
This book, and everything else, is for you.
—M.G.

Bird:
an animal that
has feathers
covering all or
most of its body

Sparrow, Eagle, Penguin, and Seagull

What Is a Bird?

by Brian P. Cleary

illustrations by Martin Goneau

M Millbrook Press • Minneapolis

Birds are feathered animals.
Their mouths are bills or beaks.

And they can live most anywhere:

in deserts,

woods,

or creeks.

Every type of **bird** breathes air.
They all have just two legs.

Their forearms are their wings, and
baby **birds** are born from eggs.

Feathers serve to block the sun and keep **birds** warm and dry.

They help them in attracting mates.
And plus, they help them fly!

Feathers can help **birds** blend in.
They keep some safe and sound

by hiding them from predators
in flight and on the ground.

Sniff

Birds are called warm-blooded 'cause they make their bodies' heat.

12

This keeps their temperature just right—
a trait that's pretty neat.

Whether they eat nectar, fish,
or algae, bugs, or seeds,

each **bird** has a beak or bill

that suits its feeding needs.

All **birds** walk and most can fly.

A few, like ducks, can swim.

HA HA HA

Some hang out in nooks and nests.
Some go out on a limb.

Doves and pigeons are among the quietest of birds.

Some **birds,**
like the hummingbird,
throughout their lives are small.

The largest is the ostrich, which can grow to nine feet tall.

Can you name any **birds** that are unable to take flight?

The kiwi and the ostrich and the penguin all are right.

What **bird** dines on little mice?
Has three eyelids—not two?

If you should give some pigeons food, they'll often come right at you.

And later,
they won't
use a toilet—

GENERAL
P. BODY

they'll just find a statue!

Fly to our back pages now.
You're sure to learn more things

about the many types of **birds**—
then you'll have earned your **wings!**

So, what is a **bird**?
Do you know?

An animal is a bird if . . .
- it has feathers covering all or most of its body

In addition, all birds . . .

- breathe air;
- are born from eggs;
- have a backbone (they're vertebrates);
- are warm-blooded.
  That means they
  make their own
  body heat. So their
  bodies' temperature
  always stays about
  the same.

And most birds . . .

- fly.

Find activities, games, and more at
www.brianpcleary.com

ABOUT THE AUTHOR & ILLUSTRATOR

BRIAN P. CLEARY is the author of the Words Are CATegorical®, Math Is CATegorical®, Adventures in Memory™, Sounds Like Reading®, and Food Is CATegorical™ series, as well as several picture books and poetry books. He lives in Cleveland, Ohio.

MARTIN GONEAU is the illustrator of the Food Is CATegorical™ series. He lives in Trois-Rivières, Québec.

Text copyright © 2013 by Brian P. Cleary
Illustrations copyright © 2013 by Lerner Publishing Group, Inc.

Millbrook Press
A division of Lerner Publishing Group, Inc.
241 First Avenue North
Minneapolis, MN 55401 U.S.A.

Website address: www.lernerbooks.com

Feather Background: © Jeremy Richards/Dreamstime.com.

Main body text set in Chauncy Decaf Medium 35/44. Typeface provided by the Chank Company.

Library of Congress Cataloging-in-Publication Data

Cleary, Brian P., 1959-
    Sparrow, eagle, penguin, and seagull : what is a bird? / by Brian P. Cleary ; illustrated by Martin Goneau.
        p.   cm. — (Animal groups are CATegorical)
    ISBN 978-0-7613-6207-4 (lib. bdg. : alk. paper)
    1. Birds—Juvenile literature. I. Goneau, Martin, ill. II. Title.
QL676.2.C54 2013
598—dc23   2011050203

Manufactured in the United States of America
1 – DP – 7/15/2012